I0796519

This book is dedicated to the memory of my father-in-law—Dr. Albert C. Antoine, a NASA chemist who developed rocket fuels for spacecraft—and my mother-in-law—Mrs. June Sallee Antoine, an educator and arts advocate.

LIFTOFF!

How the Apollo Moon Missions Made Alma Thomas's Art Soar

NINA CREWS

Millbrook Press
Minneapolis

Dawn breaks on a new day.

Pink petals, yellow butterflies, green leaves—Alma Thomas's backyard dances with color in the morning breeze.

It's a beautiful day, but Alma will go inside soon. She's eager to get to work. She has plans for something new—a painting about the astronauts and the Moon.

A year earlier, on May 18, 1969, three astronauts suited up and boarded their spacecraft, Apollo 10. They were heading on an eight-day journey to the Moon and back.

Their mission was to conduct tests before another crew of astronauts attempted the first-ever Moon landing.

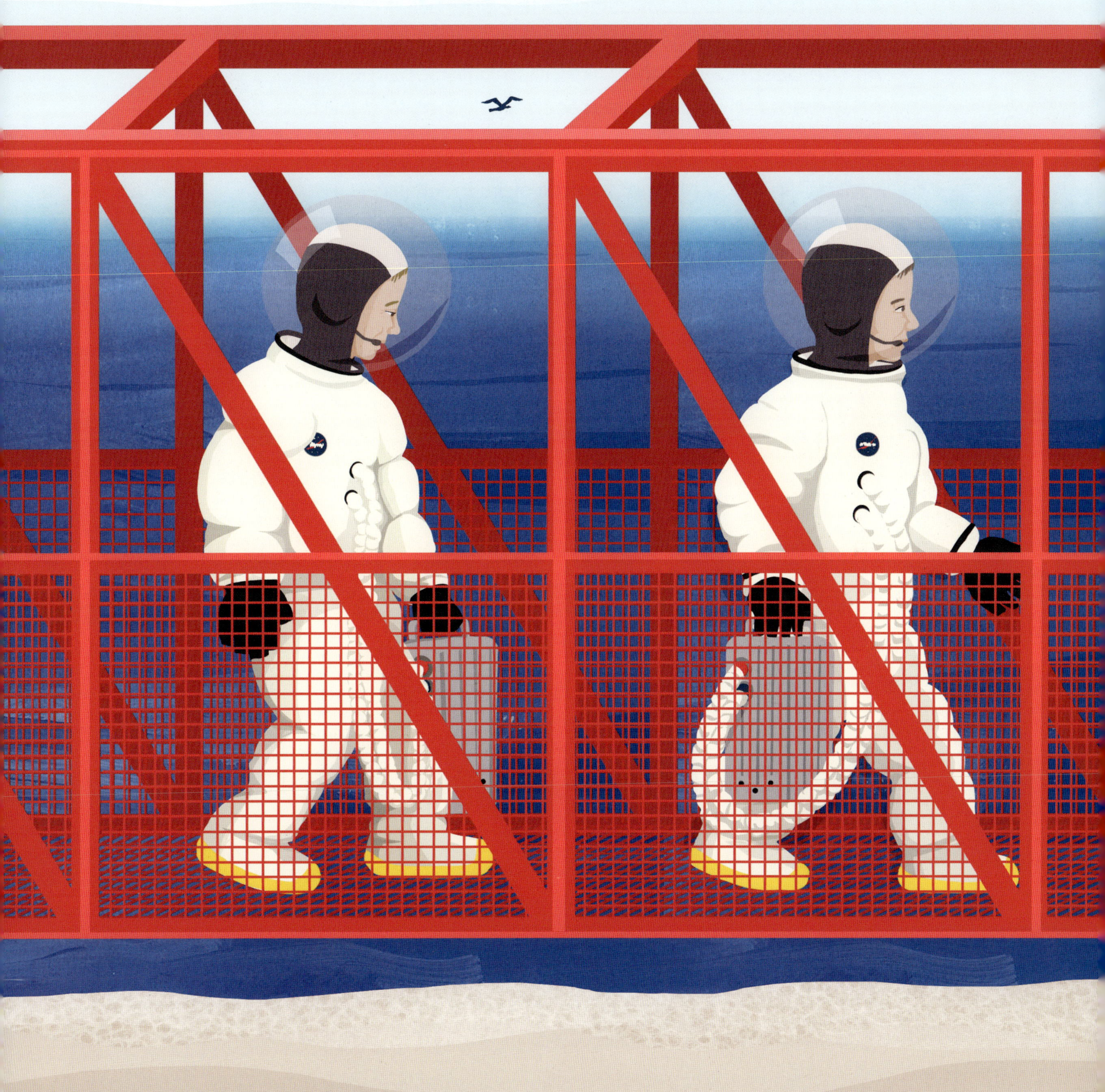

Alma Thomas is an abstract artist. She doesn't paint recognizable things like a flower or a tree or a person. As she describes it, she takes in impressions that she observes and then expresses those things in a picture.

Alma calls her style of painting "Alma's stripes." She makes dashes of bright, bold colors in straight and curved lines. She leaves a little space in between them that lets the canvas underneath show through. It is modern art. A new way of looking at the world.

"10, 9, 8, 7, 6, 5, 4—
IGNITION—3, 2, 0."

LIFTOFF!

The Apollo 10 spaceship blasted through the sky atop a 300-foot rocket. Spectators, TV crews, and reporters watched from miles away. Amazing!

Alma believes art can be "anything . . .

as long as it's beautiful."

For Alma, art can be paintings of boxes and bottles, trees and flowers, a dance called the Watusi, or the March on Washington.

Art can be the marionettes that she sculpted, painted, and sewed with her students at Shaw Junior High School.

Five hours into the flight, the astronauts were ready to send a TV broadcast back to Earth.

"YOU OUGHT TO SEE IT UP HERE," said Thomas Stafford.

"WE'VE GOT THE WHOLE GLOBE THERE," said John Young.

All around the country and around the world, people saw what the astronauts saw 25,000 miles away. Beautiful blue planet Earth, live and in color. It was almost like being right there in the spaceship with them. This was a new way of looking at the world.

Alma has made dozens of sketches and tested her colors.

She's prepared a large canvas with a coat of white paint, a four-by-four-foot space for something new.

Three days after launch, the spacecraft entered lunar orbit and the astronauts sent another TV broadcast.

"Here's hello from the five of us from on Apollo 10 . . . Here's Tom Stafford . . . John Young . . . and yours truly, Gene Cernan.

"Are you still with us? . . . Okay. That's the three of us. Here's the other two on Apollo 10, your friendly Charlie Brown and our ever loving companion, Snoopy."

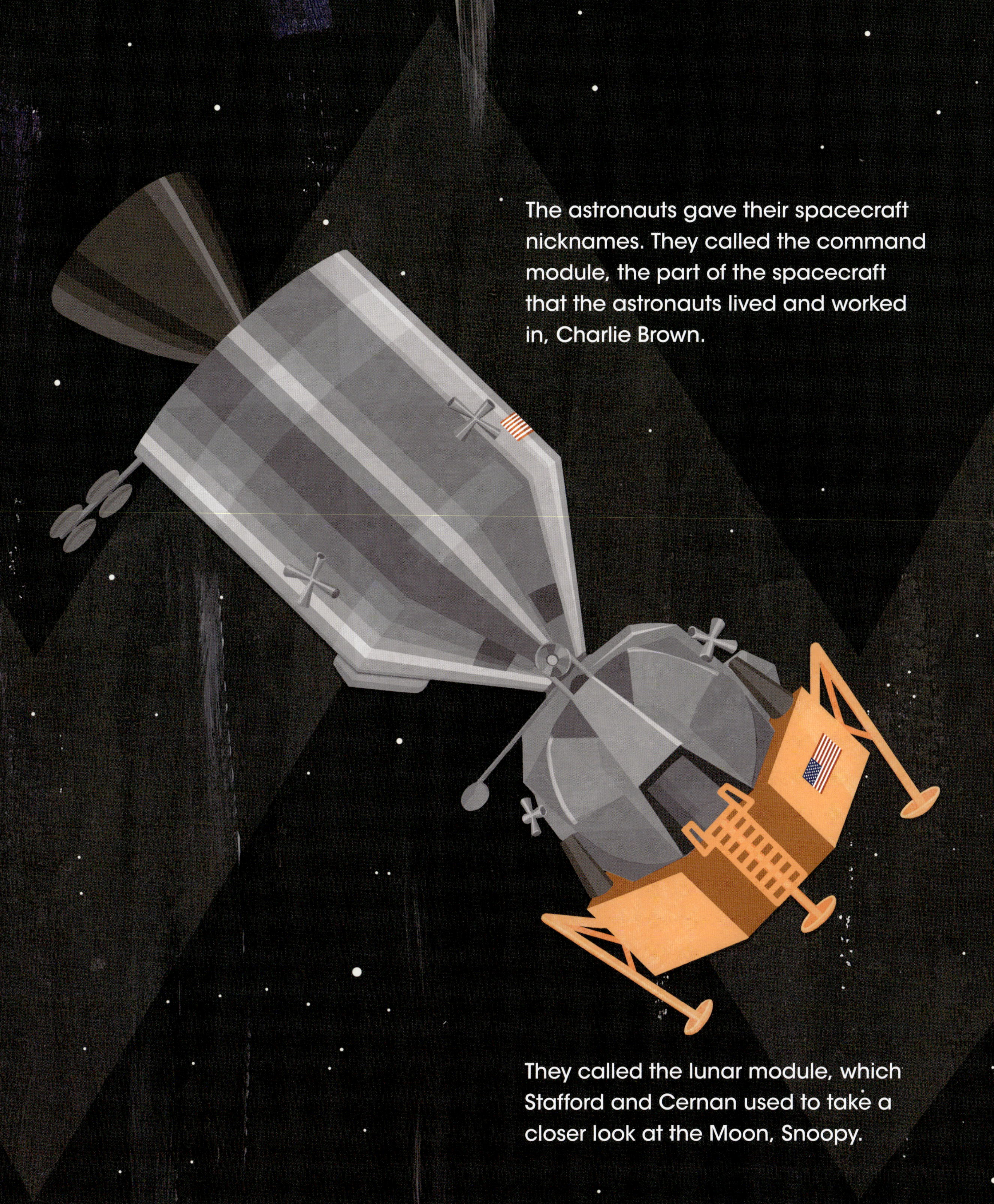

The astronauts gave their spacecraft nicknames. They called the command module, the part of the spacecraft that the astronauts lived and worked in, Charlie Brown.

They called the lunar module, which Stafford and Cernan used to take a closer look at the Moon, Snoopy.

Alma leans forward with her paintbrush, placing her marks carefully.

She puts plum-colored dashes at the left edge of a big circle.

One stroke follows another down in a line to form the circle's edge.

Next to that, purple dashes.

And after that, dashes of deep aquamarine blue.

After the astronauts settled the ship into orbit around the Moon, Stafford and Cernan climbed into Snoopy, the lunar module, to conduct a test flight. They checked that all the equipment worked as it should and made notes on anything that didn't. They took measurements and filmed and photographed the lunar surface. They scouted good landing sites for the next mission—Apollo 11.

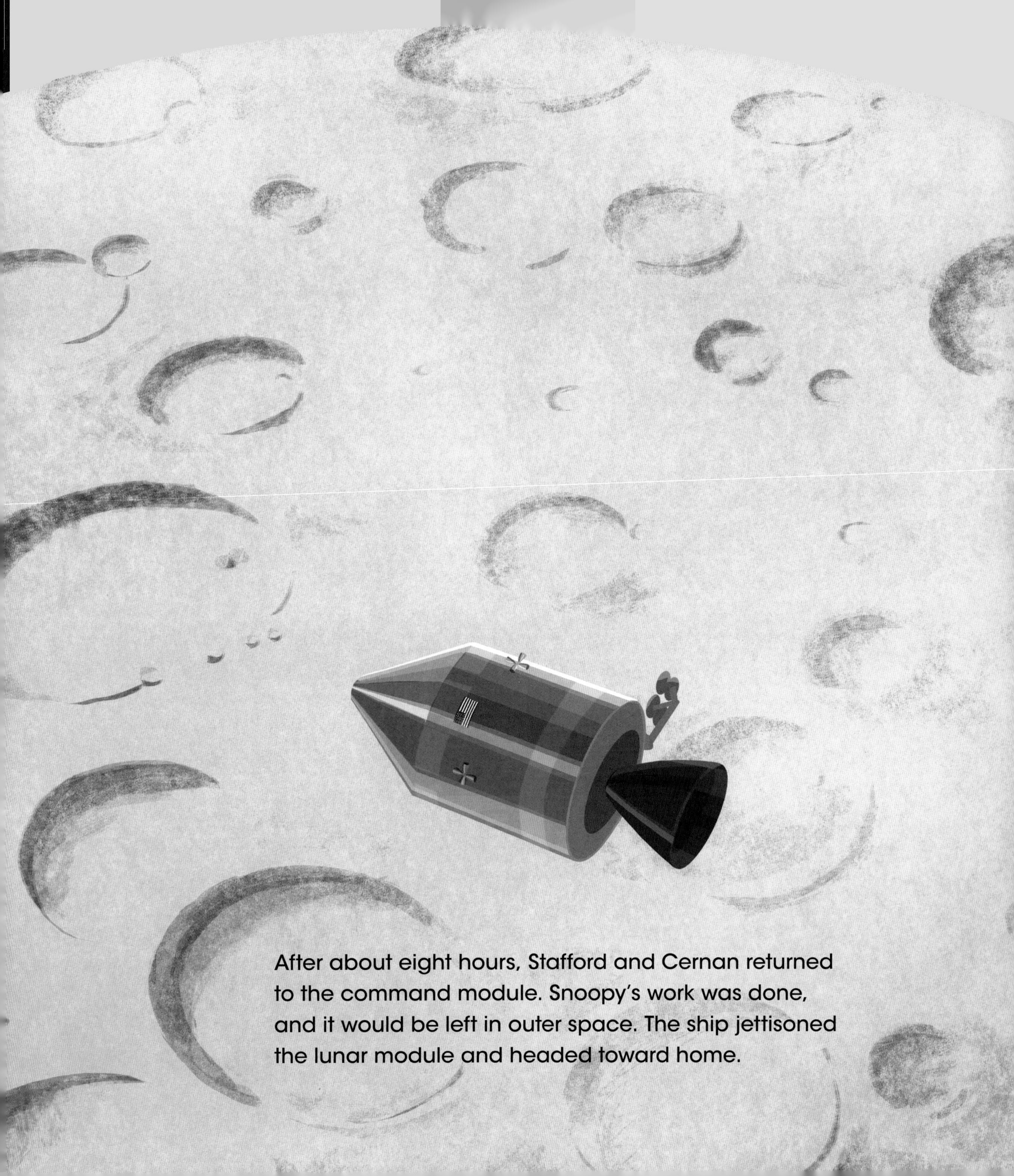

After about eight hours, Stafford and Cernan returned to the command module. Snoopy's work was done, and it would be left in outer space. The ship jettisoned the lunar module and headed toward home.

The colors pop and glow. They shimmy, shake, and dance across the canvas. Slowly, steadily, the idea that Alma had in her mind takes shape. She's flying with Snoopy in an ebony-black sky.

Is that planet Earth in the distance?

Eight days after liftoff, the Apollo 10 command module returned to Earth, splashing down safely in the deepest blue sea. Mission accomplished.

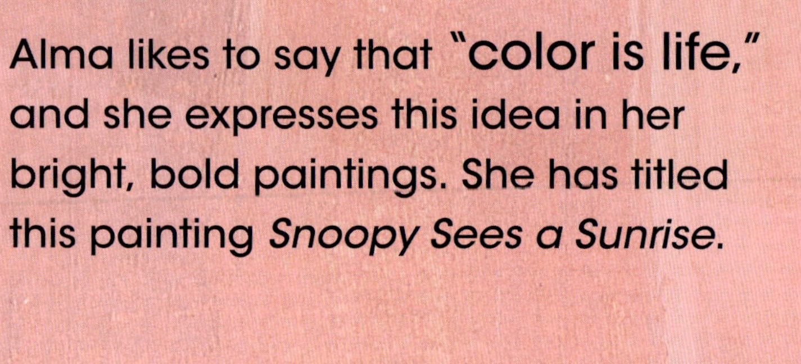

Alma likes to say that "color is life," and she expresses this idea in her bright, bold paintings. She has titled this painting *Snoopy Sees a Sunrise*.

The astronauts had identified Earth's continents and oceans for the TV audience. Alma has painted her impression of this scene in Alma's stripes.

And while the astronauts described Earth as being surrounded by the blackest black, Alma shows something different. She wraps her circle in pink, like the morning sky.

THE NEWS
25¢
VOLUME LXII
MONDAY, JULY 21, 1969
MEN WALK ON THE MOON

Dawn welcoming the future and
the possibility of something new.

More About Alma Thomas

Alma Thomas in 1966 with two of the paintings from her solo exhibition at Howard University Gallery of Art.

Alma Thomas was born in 1891 in Columbus, Georgia. The oldest of four daughters, she was raised in a family that valued education and the arts. They lived in a quiet neighborhood with a flower-filled garden. Thomas's parents regularly hosted evening gatherings of Black social clubs where they would discuss literature, history, and art. Her mother, Amelia, was a graduate of the Tuskegee Institute and a dressmaker. Her father, John, owned a successful saloon for a number of years. When Thomas was a teenager, the family moved from their home in Columbus to Washington, DC, for educational opportunities for their daughters and for the safety of their family. In 1906, white mobs had attacked Black residents in Atlanta, and in Columbus, Black people were routinely threatened with violence as unfair segregation laws were put in place. Upon their arrival in DC, Alma's mother instructed her to shake the Georgia dirt off her feet. There was no looking back, and there was no going back. Her parents bought a house in the Logan Circle neighborhood, which was predominantly Black. Thomas would live there for the rest of her life.

As a teenager, Thomas took art classes at Armstrong Manual Training High School, and she described the art room as "a beautiful place, just where I belonged." After high school, she became a kindergarten teacher. At the age of thirty, she enrolled at Howard University, and three years later, she became the first female graduate of the university's new art department.

After college, Thomas began teaching art to students at Shaw Junior High School. She did more than just teach her students the fundamentals of painting and drawing during the thirty-five years that she worked there. She started art clubs, taking her students to nearby museums, and she brought original art to the school. Thomas started a Negro History Week so that Shaw students would learn about important African Americans. She created a marionette club that brought plays to Black children throughout the city. She also continued her own education, receiving a master's degree in arts education from Teachers College, Columbia University, and studying art both at American University and privately with painters such as Jacob Kainen.

Thomas was involved with the Washington, DC, art scene throughout her life. In 1943, she became vice president of the Barnett Aden Gallery, a Black-owned space that exhibited new work by artists from diverse backgrounds. She was friends with many local artists including David Driskell, Loïs Mailou Jones, and Sam Gilliam. She began showing her work in galleries in the 1950s and had her first solo exhibition in 1966. In 1972, she became the first African American woman to have a solo exhibit at the Whitney Museum of American Art in New York City, an important breakthrough for representation in the art world.

Thomas lived a simple life. She never married. Her painting studio was in her kitchen, and behind it, she filled a garden with flowers. She was inspired by nature and the technological inventions of the twentieth century, flying in her imagination as she painted abstracted overhead views of gardens and scenes from outer space. Her most successful years as a painter were when she was in her seventies and eighties, and she remained committed to her work despite terrible bouts of arthritis. Alma Thomas died in 1978 at the age of eighty-six.

More About the Apollo Missions

In an address to Congress in 1961, President John F. Kennedy said, "I believe this nation should commit itself to achieving the goal, before this decade is out, of landing a man on the Moon and returning him safely to the earth." What inspired him to make such a bold statement? At that time, the US government was competing with the Soviet Union to achieve technological breakthroughs, and the Soviets were ahead in space. The Soviet Union was a country that consisted of Russia and fourteen other republics. The two countries had become rivals after the end of World War II in 1945, and the decades that followed were known as the Cold War. This period was marked by hostile relations rather than direct fighting, and each country strove to have greater influence over the rest of the world. Achieving important "firsts" in space travel gave each nation a chance to claim it was superior. Space technology had other uses too. Satellites could be used for spying, and rockets had the potential to launch missiles. In 1957, the Soviet Union launched the world's first satellite, Sputnik, into low Earth orbit. In 1961, a month before Kennedy's speech to Congress, Soviet Cosmonaut Yuri Gagarin orbited Earth in a Soviet spaceship.

A relatively new government agency, the National Aeronautics and Space Agency (NASA), was in charge of achieving President Kennedy's goal. The work progressed in stages, and each milestone reached was cause for celebration. In 1961, Alan Shepard became the first American to fly in space in the Mercury spacecraft Freedom 7. In 1962, John Glenn became the first American to orbit the Earth in the Friendship 7 spacecraft. In 1968, the Apollo 7 spacecraft sent the first TV broadcasts back to Earth during its eleven-day flight. At the end of that year, Apollo 8 traveled to the Moon, orbiting it several times before returning back to Earth two days after Christmas. The Apollo 10 mission featured in this book has been called the "dress rehearsal" for the moon landing. Two months later, on July 20, 1969, Apollo 11 astronauts Neil Armstrong and Buzz Aldrin became the first people to walk on the Moon.

Reaching the Moon was an inspiring goal. The space program also created huge opportunities for many Americans because this enormous and complicated task involved hundreds of thousands of people. Astronauts, engineers, mathematicians, physicists, chemists, computer scientists, seamstresses, mechanics, truck drivers, janitors, and countless others were hired to make this dream a reality. The space program got started during a time of progress for the Civil Rights Movement. Activists worked with Presidents John F. Kennedy and Lyndon B. Johnson to ensure NASA would recruit and hire African American employees. A number of Black Americans with training in math and the sciences were able to get skilled jobs that might have been denied to them by private companies. Hiring a diverse group of workers at NASA helped pave the way for integrating other workplaces across the country. One African American test pilot, Ed Dwight, participated in the early astronaut training rounds, but he was not part of the final selection.

The last Apollo mission returned to Earth on December 19, 1972. Astronauts spent three days on the lunar surface conducting moonwalks and collecting samples. After that time, NASA shifted its focus to other projects and did not send another mission to the Moon until the 1990s. Four other countries, the Soviet Union, China, India, and Japan, have landed uncrewed spacecraft on the Moon, and NASA has plans for human exploration in the next few years through its Artemis program.

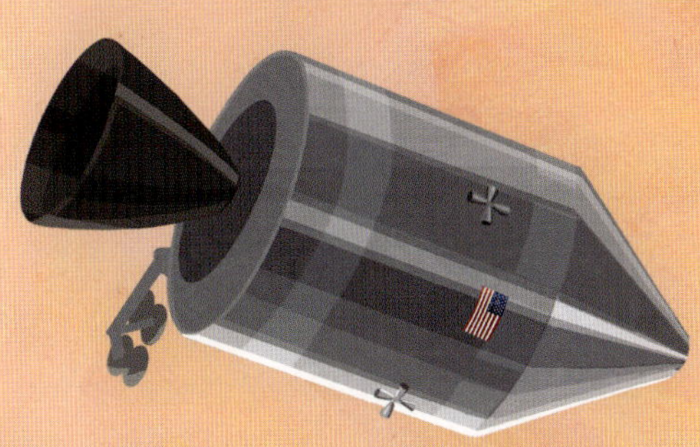

More About Snoopy and the Moon

The cartoonist Charles Schulz published his first *Peanuts* cartoon in October 1950, and the strip appeared in 7 newspapers. By the end of the decade, Peanuts was a huge success, appearing daily in more than 350 US newspapers and 40 foreign papers. The cartoons were published in books, and the characters were used in ads and greeting cards, and sold as toys. In 1968, with Schulz's permission and involvement, Snoopy became NASA's safety mascot. Snoopy appeared on NASA badges, banners, and pins given to staff as an award encouraging mission safety. The Apollo 10 astronauts brought a picture of Snoopy with them in their spacecraft. Schulz also created a series of comic strips depicting Snoopy traveling in his doghouse to the Moon. The cartoons were published in March 1969, so Snoopy got there a few months ahead of the Apollo 11 crew.

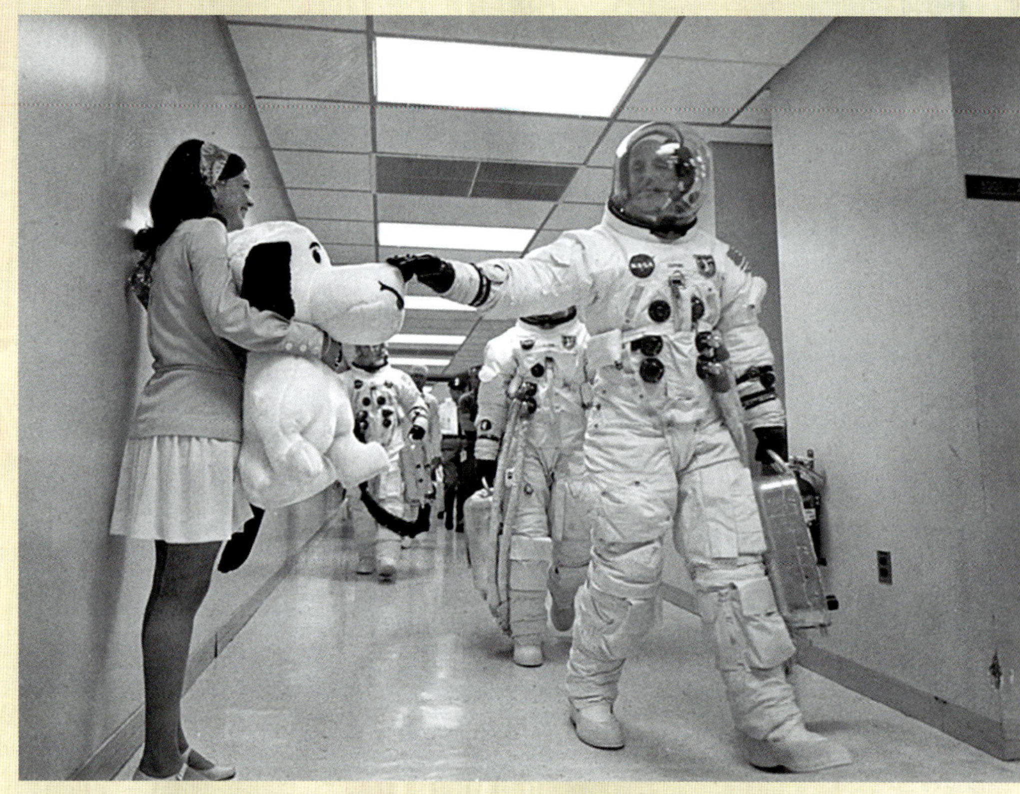

Apollo 10 commander Thomas Stafford pats Snoopy's nose as the crew heads to the launchpad at Kennedy Space Center on May 18, 1969.

Source Notes

"10, 9, 8 . . . 3, 2, 0.": W. David Woods, Robin Wheeler, and Ian Roberts, trans. eds., "Apollo 10, Day 1, part 1," CapCom, 000:00:00, National Aeronautics and Space Administration, last updated August 1, 2022, https://www.nasa.gov/history/afj/ap10fj/as10-day1-pt1.html.

"anything . . . as long as it's beautiful.": Alma Thomas, quoted by David L. Shirey, "At 77, She's Made It to the Whitney," *New York Times*, May 4, 1972, https://www.nytimes.com/1972/05/04/archives/at-77-shes-made-it-to-the-whitney.html.

"You ought to see it up here,": W. David Woods, Robin Wheeler, and Ian Roberts, trans. eds., "Apollo 10, Day 1, part 5," Thomas Stafford, 005:07:01, National Aeronautics and Space Administration, last updated August 1, 2022, https://www.nasa.gov/history/afj/ap10fj/as10-day1-pt5-lmext-sivb-sep.html.

"We've got the whole globe there,": John Young, "Apollo 10, Day 1, part 5," 005:07:03.

"Here's hello from . . . our ever loving companion, Snoopy.": W. David Woods, Robin Wheeler, and Ian Roberts, trans. eds., "Apollo 10, Day 3, part 11," Eugene Cernan, 053:37:11-053:37:39, National Aeronautics and Space Administration, last updated August 1, 2022, https://www.nasa.gov/history/afj/ap10fj/as10-day3-pt11.html.

"color is life,": Alma Thomas, Whitney Museum of American Art exhibit brochure, 1972, New York, 2.

"a beautiful place, just where I belonged.": Eleanor Munro, *Originals: American Women Artists* (Simon and Schuster, 1979), 193.

"I believe this nation . . . safely to the earth.": John F. Kennedy, "Excerpt from an Address Before a Joint Session of Congress," JFK Library, May 25, 1961, https://www.jfklibrary.org/asset-viewer/archives/tnc-200-2.

Bibliography

Alma W. Thomas Resources

Feman, Seth, and Jonathan Frederick Walz. *Alma W. Thomas: Everything Is Beautiful*. Columbus Museum, 2021.

Hodge-Thorne, Cynthia. "The Politics of Space: Alma Thomas and Race Relations in 1960s America." MA diss. American University, 2019. http://hdl.handle.net/1961/auislandora:84411.

Munro, Eleanor. "Alma W. Thomas." In *Originals: American Women Artists*. Simon and Schuster, 1979.

Thomas, Alma. "Alma Thomas Papers circa 1894–2001." Archives of American Art, Smithsonian Institution, Washington, DC. Accessed October 4, 2023. https://www.aaa.si.edu/collections/alma-thomas-papers-9241.

Thomas, Alma. Solo exhibition. Whitney Museum of American Art, 1972. Artist statement and exhibition catalog.

Apollo Moon Mission Resources

Alaina. "Snoopy, Charlie Brown and Apollo 10." *The Payload Blog*, May 16, 2019. https://www.kennedyspacecenter.com/blog/snoopy-charlie-brown-and-apollo-10.

Dickinson, David. "Astronomers Might Have Found Apollo 10's 'Snoopy' Module." Sky & Telescope, June 14, 2019. https://skyandtelescope.org/astronomy-news/astronomers-might-have-found-apollo-10-snoopy-module.

Fishman, Charles. *One Giant Leap: The Impossible Mission That Flew Us to the Moon*. Simon and Schuster, 2019.

Stafford, Thomas P. "NASA Johnson Space Center Oral History Project Edited Oral History Transcript." Interview by William Vantine. October 15, 1997. https://historycollection.jsc.nasa.gov/JSCHistoryPortal/history/oral_histories/StaffordTP/StaffordTP_10-15-97.htm.

Woods, W. David, Robin Wheeler, and Ian Roberts, trans. eds. "Apollo 10 Flight Journal." National Aeronautics and Space Administration. Last updated August 1, 2022. https://history.nasa.gov/afj/ap10fj/index.html.

Suggested Further Reading

Becker, Helaine. *Counting On Katherine: How Katherine Johnson Saved Apollo 13*. Illustrated by Dow Phumiruk. Christy Ottaviano Books, 2018.

Floca, Brian. *Moonshot: The Flight of Apollo 11*. Atheneum Books for Young Readers, 2009.

Greenberg, Jan, and Sandra Jordan. *Action Jackson*. Illustrated by Robert Andrew Parker. Roaring Brook, 2002.

Harvey, Jeanne Walker. *Ablaze with Color: A Story of Painter Alma Thomas*. Illustrated by Loveis Wise. HarperCollins, 2022.

Rocco, John. *How We Got to the Moon: An Illustrated Guide to One of the Most Challenging, Dangerous and Astounding Achievements in Human History*. Crown Books for Young Readers, 2020.

Millbrook Press™
An imprint of Lerner Publishing Group, Inc.
241 First Avenue North
Minneapolis, MN 55401 USA

For reading levels and more information, look up this title at www.lernerbooks.com.

Photo credits: Alma Thomas, *Snoopy Sees a Sunrise*, 1970, © 2024 Estate of Alma Thomas (Courtesy of the Hart Family)/Artists Rights Society, New York, image provided by Smithsonian National Air and Space Museum, p. 29; Ellsworth Davis/The Washington Post via Getty Image, p. 30; NASA, p. 32.

Designed by Danielle Carnito and Nina Crews.
Main body text set in ITC Avant Garde Gothic Std.
Typeface provided by Adobe Systems.

The illustrations in this book were created using Adobe Photoshop and include scans of handmade textures and painted elements.

Library of Congress Cataloging-in-Publication Data

Names: Crews, Nina, author, illustrator. | Crews, Nina, illustrator.
Title: Liftoff! : how the Apollo moon missions made Alma Thomas's art soar / Nina Crews.
Description: Minneapolis : Millbrook Press, [2025] | Includes bibliographical references. | Audience: Ages 6–10 | Audience: Grades 2–3 | Summary: "In this fascinating STEAM-themed true story, author and illustrator Nina Crews highlights how the Apollo astronauts gave people a new way of looking at the world and inspired modern artist Alma Thomas" —Provided by publisher.
Identifiers: LCCN 2024054187 (print) | LCCN 2024054188 (ebook) | ISBN 9798765643471 (library binding) | ISBN 9798765682531 (epub)
Subjects: LCSH: Thomas, Alma—Juvenile literature. | Project Apollo (U.S.)—In art—Juvenile literature.
Classification: LCC ND237.T5517 C74 2025 (print) | LCC ND237.T5517 (ebook) | DDC 759.13—dc23/eng/20241230

LC record available at https://lccn.loc.gov/2024054187
LC ebook record available at https://lccn.loc.gov/2024054188

Manufactured in Guang Dong, China by Dream Colour Printing
1-1012027-52387-3/18/2025